DATE DUE

DEMCO 128-8155

H. G. WELLS

H. G. WELLS

Christopher Martin

ROURKE ENTERPRISES, INC.
Vero Beach, Florida 32964

Life and Works

Jane Austen
The Brontës
Thomas Hardy
Ernest Hemingway
D. H. Lawrence
Katherine Mansfield
George Orwell
Shakespeare
H. G. Wells
Virginia Woolf

Cover illustration by David Armitage

Text © 1989 Rourke Enterprises, Inc.
PO Box 3328, Vero Beach, Florida 32964

Library of Congress Cataloging-in-Publication Data

Martin, Christopher, 1952–
    H. G. Wells/by Christopher Martin.
       p.   cm.—(Life and works)
    Bibliography: p.
    Includes index.
    Summary: A biography of the English author who has been
called the first great science fiction writer, with a discussion of
his works .
    ISBN 0–86592–297–7
    1. Wells, H. G. (Herbert George). 1866–1946—Juvenile
literature.   2. Novelists, English—20th century—Biography—
Juvenile literature.   [1. Wells, H. G. (Herbert George),
1866–1946. 2. Authors, English.] I. Title. II. Series.
PR5776.M35   1988
823′ .912—dc19
[B]
[92]   88–15650
                                           CIP
                                         AC

Manufactured in England

Contents

1 The Ugly Duckling

H. G. Wells was a poor draper's assistant who rose in society to move as an equal among the great figures of his time. He described himself as the ugly duckling who discovered himself to be a swan. Born into the cramped life of the Victorian lower middle class, he had to struggle fiercely to fulfill himself. He was, he said, like "a creature trying to find its way out of a prison into which it has fallen." Despite formidable obstacles, he won himself a good scientific education, and eventually, fame and fortune.

H. G. Wells at the height of his early fame, when The War of the Worlds *first appeared in 1898.*

Herbert George Wells was born on September 21, 1866. The circumstances of his birth were not promising: a "needy, shabby home" behind his father's unsuccessful china shop in Bromley, Kent. His parents had met as servants at Uppark, a large country house near Midhurst in Sussex. Sarah, his mother, had been a lady's maid; Joseph, his father, a gardener. After their marriage in 1855, the Wellses, like so many others in nineteenth-century England, had drifted from country to town, finally settling in Bromley, where they bought from a cousin the run-down china business that was always to be "a miserable half-living."

Wells's parents, Sarah and Joseph, were Victorian servants turned shopkeepers.

Bromley's main street in 1905: Atlas House was on the left where Medhursts now stands.

Herbert was the fourth and youngest of the Wells children; Frances, who died young, Frank and Fred came before him. Delicate in health and sent, his mother thought, to replace the dead daughter she had adored, he was inevitably rather spoiled. "Woe betide if toys his highness wanted were denied him," recalled his brother Frank. He was precocious, too. His mother soon taught him his letters, and his first written word, of the many millions he was to write, was "butter," traced out on a window pane over his mother's writing.

The Wells home was full of tension. The marriage was not a happy one. Sarah lived a life of grim resentment of her feckless husband, and became a household drudge, struggling to maintain what her son called the "gaunt, impossible" house. Wells remembered his mother's hands, "so grimy, so needleworn, so misshapen by toil." Joseph, a model for his son's later creation, Mr. Polly, was a listless, ineffectual tradesman, lounging at the door of his shop. Although Bromley was a rapidly growing suburb of London, with good opportunities for trade, Joseph allowed his business to dwindle. Whenever he could, he escaped to play cricket. He was a skilled player, good enough to play for Kent. Despite his father's inadequacy and bad temper, Wells loved him. He saw a "vein of silent poetry" in Joseph, who as a youth had liked to stay outdoors half the summer night, simply staring at the stars.

His mother's attempts to instill her prim religious beliefs into her son largely failed. He came to think of God as "an old sneak . . . with an all-seeing eye." Nevertheless, the pictures of Hell in one of the family books affected him strongly, and his mother's views on the Last Judgment and the New Jerusalem evolved into key

Wells as a bright ten-year-old schoolboy in 1876.

elements of his science-fiction and Utopian novels. From his father, Wells inherited his rich imagination. When he was seven, he broke his leg in an accident and was laid up for several weeks. This interlude became a feast of reading books of all kinds, either borrowed by his father from the library or sent in by neighbors. Wells loved exotic facts: tales of strange countries, curious animals and great battles. His imagination was fired by an old atlas that showed large unexplored regions; his fears by the gorilla in Wood's *Natural History*, which in dreams followed him about the house. From the political cartoons in *Punch* magazine, he gained his first ideas of politics and international affairs.

His mother had an exact sense of the family's social position at the lower end of the lower middle class, and combined "the deference of the servant with a jealously guarded respectability above the common herd." This made her choose a private school, the so-called Bromley Academy, for her sons instead of the working-class "National" church elementary school. Wells, like Charles Dickens, wrote bitterly about the fraudulent private-enterprise schooling of the Victorian era. He satirized his own education in the picture of Mr. Woodrow's Cavendish Academy in his novel *Kipps* (1905):

> The memories Kipps carried from that school into after-life were set in an atmosphere of stuffiness and mental muddle, and included countless pictures of sitting on creaking forms, bored and idle; of blot licking and the taste of ink ... of the slimy surface of the laboured slates ... of standing up in class and being hit suddenly and unreasonably for imaginary misbehaviour ... Mr. Woodrow sat inanimate at his desk, heedless of school affairs, staring in front of him at unseen things. At times his face was utterly inane; at times it had an expression of stagnant amazement, as if he saw before his eyes with pitiless clearness the dishonour and mischief of his being.
>
> (*Kipps*, Ch. 1)

Outside school his imagination expanded. On solitary walks he devised war fantasies, stimulated by reading *Boys of England*, an early comic. In his autobiography (1934) he recalled how outwardly he was "a small, rather undernourished boy, meanly clad and whistling

Punch *cartoons, like this by Sir John Tenniel showing Disraeli and Queen Victoria, gave Wells his first ideas about the political world.*

"NEW CROWNS FOR OLD ONES!"

(ALADDIN *adapted.*)

detestably between his teeth." Passersby could not have suspected that "a phantom staff pranced about me . . . to shift the guns and fire upon those houses below . . . Kings and presidents, and the great of the earth, came to salute my saving wisdom." He wrote an illustrated story, "The Desert Daisy," in similar vein. Such violent daydreams became a permanent part of his imagination.

The Battle.

Wells's drawing of a battle scene from his violent boyhood fantasy story, "The Desert Daisy."

Sarah Wells used this room when she became housekeeper at Uppark House in Sussex in 1880.

Life became even harder for the Wells family after 1877, when Joseph broke his leg in a fall in the backyard, thus putting an end to his cricket activity and the extra income it provided. For two years Sarah struggled on. Then the family broke apart. In 1880 Sarah was suddenly invited to become housekeeper at Uppark, which her old mistress, Frances Fetherstonhaugh, had now inherited. At the same time her son Herbert, then aged fourteen, was sent to follow his brothers into the textile, or drapery, trade.

"Almost as unquestioning as her belief in Our Father ... was her belief in drapers," wrote Wells of his mother. "To wear a black coat and tie behind a counter was the best of all possible lots attainable by man – at our social level." As an apprentice "living in" at a respectable shop in Windsor, Wells worked 13 hours a day, six days a week. He slept in a seedy dormitory and ate in an

Rodgers & Denyers 25 High Street
Sunday July 4th 1880

My dear Mother

Here I am sitting in my bed room after the fatigues of the day etc. Cough slightly better & I am tolerably comfortable. I give you an account of one days work to give you an idea what I have to do.

Morning

We sleep 4 together viz 3 apprentices & 1 of the hands in one room (of course in separate beds)
We lay in bed until 7.30 when a bell rings & we jump up & put trousers slippers socks & jacket on over nightgown & hurry down & dust the shop etc
about 8.15 we hurry upstairs & dress & wash for breakfast.
At 8.30 we go into a sort of vault underground (lit by gas) & have breakfast. After breakfast I am in the shop & desk till dinner at 1 (we have dinner underground as well as breakfast) & then work till tea (which we have in the same place) & then go on to supper at 8.30 at which time work is done & we may then go out until 10.30 at which hour the apprentices are obliged to be in the house.
I don't like the place much it is not at all like home
Give love to Dad & give the Cats my best respects
I'm rather tired of being indoors but

I went to Clewer Church & then on to Surley which I found much better than I used to think it in fact it's a perfect heaven to R&D's
I'm rather tired so excuse further writing
yours
Al G Wells
N.B. My washing will be 1/- a quarter

A letter written in 1880 from Wells to his mother describing the harsh conditions of life as a draper's assistant "living in" at a Windsor shop.

15

underground dining room. He detested the work. What the boyhood humiliations of working in a factory were to Dickens, the life of the "shopman" was to Wells.

It's not a particularly honest nor a particularly useful trade ... There's no freedom and no leisure – seven to eight-thirty every day in the week; don't leave much to live on, does it? – real workmen laugh at us, and educated chaps like bank clerks and solicitors' clerks look down on us. You look respectable outside, and inside you are packed in dormitories like convicts, fed on bread and butter, and bullied like slaves. You're just superior enough to feel that you're not superior ... That's drapery ... We're too – sort of shabby genteel to rise. Our coats and cuffs might get crumpled ...

(*The Wheels of Chance*, Ch. 26, 1896)

'Ow are they to get shops of their own? They 'aven't any Capital! How's a draper's shopman to save up five hundred pounds even? I tell you it can't be done. You got to stick to Cribs until it's over. I tell you we're in a blessed drain-pipe, and we've got to crawl along it till we die ...

(*Kipps*, Ch. 2)

His only pleasure in Windsor was escape on Sundays to nearby Surly Hall, a riverside inn (the original of the Potwell Inn in *Mr. Polly*) kept by an uncle. There he boated and sang with his girl cousins, and there too he first read Dickens's novels, which were to have such an influence on his own work. Back at the shop, he daydreamed at his desk: "Despatch riders came head-long from dreamland, brooking no denial from the shop walker. 'Is General Bert Wells here? The Prussians have landed...'" Scandal grew about his listlessly kept accounts and he was asked to leave.

He took refuge at Uppark with his mother, in the servants' quarters "below stairs." The weeks he spent in the mansion deeply impressed him. In *Tono-Bungay* (1909) he presents, in the picture of Bladesover House, a striking vision of life at Uppark as he saw it then, with an acute sense of the pathos of the dying "upstairs-downstairs" social order of the country house, where ranks of servants waited on "her Leddyship ... shrivelled, garrulous ... a thing of black silks and a golden chain." Later he came to admire certain aspects of the rural gentry's way of life:

Within these households, behind a screen of deer-park and park wall and sheltered service, men could talk, think, and write at their leisure. . . . Out of such houses came the Royal Society, the first museums and laboratories and picture galleries, gentle manners, good writing, and nearly all that is worthwhile in our civilization today.

(*Experiment in Autobiography,*
Vol. 1, Ch. 3, 1934)

The west front of Uppark House. Wells resented the upper classes as a boy but later came to admire the creative possibilities of country-house life.

Wells came to see the life of the cultivated, thinking élite as an ideal in his Utopian visions.

During this Uppark interlude of 1880–81 and later visits there, he seized the chance to borrow, from the Fetherstonhaugh library, books that were to influence him throughout his life: Tom Paine's *The Rights of Man*, Jonathan Swift's *Gulliver's Travels* and Plato's *Republic*. The ideas expressed in these books were startling: "Here was the amazing and heartening suggestion that the whole fabric of law, custom and worship . . . might be cast into the melting pot and made anew." In an attic beside his bedroom he found a forgotten telescope with which "on chilly but wonderful nights . . . I made my first contact with the starry heavens in a state of exaltation . . . as though I were Galileo come back to earth."

In January 1881 Wells made another start in life, as an apprentice to a pharmacist in nearby Midhurst. Knowledge of Latin was considered necessary for this trade, so he had private lessons from Horace Byatt, headmaster of the town's newly reformed grammar school. Wells astonished his teacher with his rapid grasp of ideas. But this happiness was short-lived; his mother could no longer pay the pharmacist's fees. In May, following his mother's wishes, he began again as a draper at an emporium in Southsea in Hampshire. For two more years he endured the misery, "the pinch of it all, the intolerable hours," the cries of "Get on with it, Wells! Wells, forward!" Pathetically he tried to continue his schooling, teaching himself by studying popular encyclopedias and writing outline answers to questions he set himself, such as "What is matter?" or "What is space?"

Finally he revolted against this "hell of a life," having come close to a breakdown. In 1883, he wrote to Byatt, asking for a post as assistant master at his school. When his mother resisted his plans, he simply ran away from the emporium, walked to Uppark and appeared dramatically by the field path as the servants returned from church. There Wells and his mother argued bitterly, but he decided to leave drapery for good. From this experience he deduced a guiding principle: "If life is not good enough for you, change it; never endure a way of life that is dull and dreary."

Wells became assistant master at Midhurst School, where he worked fiercely, pinning up in his room (like his own character, Mr. Lewisham) an ambitious "schema" or program of study for the next few years. By day he taught boys under Byatt's guidance; at night he sat alone with his master, preparing for the examinations set by the Science and Art Department, a government body set up in 1851 to stimulate scientific studies. Each subject pass was rewarded with money grants to teachers and with coveted certificates for pupils. So good were Wells's passes in the 1884 examinations that he received "a marvellous blue document" offering him an award to study at the Normal School of Science in South Kensington. *"Gloria in excelsis mei,"* Wells wrote to his brother Fred. "I have now become a holy, a respectable person, entitled to wear a gown ... and call myself an undergraduate of London University."

Midhurst Grammar School in Sussex, shortly after Wells left. His master, Horace Byatt, is sitting in the middle.

2
Uncertain Starts

The day in September 1884 when Wells first walked down Exhibition Road in London to enter the Normal School of Science was one of the happiest of his long life. In his novel *Love and Mr. Lewisham* (1900), Wells lovingly recreated the atmosphere of his student days. He was one of the scholarship winners, "raw, shabby, discordant, grotesquely ill-dressed," who lived in near poverty on £1 a week. They were the pioneers of a new age in which science was at last to become a respectable course of study.

T. H. Huxley, the great biologist and supporter of Charles Darwin, taught Wells in his first year at the Normal School of Science in South Kensington.

Wells as a poor scholarship student: the picture expresses his early passion for the theory of evolution.

Wells's first teacher was the great T. H. Huxley, the eminent Victorian scientist who was champion of Darwinism and of scientific education itself. Wells attended only one series of Huxley's lectures, yet he was deeply influenced by him. Huxley's passionate belief that science might sweep away all human misery gave religious doubters like Wells a new purpose in life. His first year studying biology and zoology under Huxley was, he considered, "the most educational year of my life." He worked so effectively that he won several first-class honors in his examinations.

Wells found lodgings with an aunt. On winter nights he worked by candle-light, wearing an overcoat, his feet thrust among his underlinen in a drawer to keep warm. Although his clothes grew shabby and acid-stained, he clung to his respectability with his rubber-coated, washable white collar. At his aunt's he met the "grave and lovely" Isabel, his cousin, who eventually became his first wife.

After his relative failure at South Kensington, Wells drew this mocking cartoon of himself pondering his future as a "Great Man."

Without the inspiration of Huxley (who had retired because of ill health), Wells's second and third years were less successful. He became, he said later, "thoroughly detestable ... a gaunt, shabby candidate for expulsion." As his work deteriorated, he sought compensating successes in other directions. He made a name as a brilliant speaker at the College Debating Society. He turned socialist and flaunted a red tie. Influenced by Henry George's book *Progress and Poverty*, which attacked capitalism for wasting the lives of millions of people, he sought an answer to his resentful question: "Why was everything appropriated and every advantage secured against me before I came into the world?" Cruel social contrasts were easily apparent in London during the depression of the 1880s.

> He had begun to realize certain aspects of our social order ... to feel something of the dull stress deepening to absolute wretchedness and pain, which is the colour of so much human life in modern London. One vivid contrast hung in his mind symbolical.
>
> On the one hand were the coalies ... on strike and gaunt and hungry, children begging in the black slush, and starving loungers outside a soup kitchen; and on the other, two streets further, a blazing array of crowded shops, a stirring traffic of cabs and carriages, and such a spate of spending that a tired student in leaky boots and graceless clothes hurrying home was continually impeded by the whirl of skirts and parcels.
>
> (*Love and Mr. Lewisham*, Ch. 8, 1900)

Wells and his friends savored meetings at Kelmscott House, home of the socialist artist William Morris. Wells also read widely in the college libraries. Here he found the imaginative essay by Sir Humphrey Davy, the great chemist, describing a voyage across the universe. It combined scientific theory with poetic vision and was to be a particular inspiration for Wells's later work. He began writing for the *Science Schools Journal*, a magazine he helped to found in 1886.

Mediocre results in his final examinations put an end to the hoped-for career in scientific research. In 1887 when he left the Normal School at South Kensington, his confidence collapsed. "And what is to become of me now?" he asked himself.

A brief spell of teaching in a dismal private school in north Wales ended in physical collapse – a kidney had been damaged by a kick from a loutish pupil in a soccer game. He also began to spit blood, the first sign of tuberculosis. Death seemed near.

> How this staggered me! I was full of the vast ambition of youth; I was still at the age when death is quite out of sight ... and then suddenly, with a gout of blood upon my knuckle ... this world which had been so solid grew faint and thin. I saw through it, saw his face near to my own; suddenly found him beside me, when I had been dreaming he was far away over the hills.
>
> ("How I Died: Certain Personal Matters," 1898)

He seemed, he told friends, to have "dropped out of the marching column." Yet, with stubborn determination, he returned to Uppark and recovered. It was during this period that he drafted *The Chronic Argonauts*, a first version of *The Time Machine*.

In July 1888, with a £5 note given to him by his mother as his sole resource, Wells returned to London – "that grey cold wilderness of people," as he called it – to seek his fortune. He found lodgings near the British Museum and did the rounds of the scholastic agencies, which found jobs for teachers. One evening, he later claimed, he came to his last halfpenny, but discovered next day that it was a shilling, which allowed him to eat again.

Then his luck turned. He found a post at a progressive private school in north London. He resumed work for his BSc degree and won first-class honors in 1890. He also studied teaching method with the College of Preceptors so successfully that he was invited to become a biology coach at the University Correspondence College. A period of prosperity began. "Stock Exchange Intelligence: Great boom in Wells's," he wrote to a friend. "Pace too high, though – life a bubble – smash at any moment." Wells now seemed set for a solid career in teaching. A pupil described him at that time as "somewhat below average height, not very robust in health and with evident signs of poverty. In dress, speech and manner he was plain and unvarnished, abrupt and direct with a somewhat cynical and outspoken scorn of the

When he retired from teaching, Wells wrote furiously to support his family, including his feckless clock-mender brother, Frank ("Little Clock Man").

Fat little Mother

Little Bertie writing away for dear life to get little things for all his little people sends his love to Little Clock Man and Little Daddy and Little Mother (December 5, 1894).

easy luxurious life." He contributed to the *Educational Times* and began his first published work, *A Textbook of Biology*. When his scientific essay "The Rediscovery of the Unique" (1891) was accepted by a leading journal, *The Fortnightly Review*, it seemed to be a hopeful sign, "the dove with the sprig of bay." "Is it poor Pilgrim's first glimpse of the white and shining city?" he asked a friend in a letter. The essay, a piece of scientific philosophy, concluded with a memorable image describing Victorian science:

> Science is a match that man has just got alight. He thought he was in a room – in moments of devotion, a temple – and that his light would be reflected from and display walls inscribed with wonderful secrets ... It is a curious sensation, now that the preliminary splutter is over and the flame burns up clear, to see his hands lit and just a glimpse of himself and the patch he stands on visible, and around him, in place of all that human comfort and beauty he anticipated – darkness still.

In 1888, Wells returned to London to seek his fortune. He drew this cartoon of himself looking for work.

By 1892, Wells was working as a biology lecturer. He drew this sketch of himself working in his rooms.

Dear Mother,
  You observe a doubtless familiar figure above, keeping his 26th birthday. In the background are bookshelves recently erected by your eldest, who came up here Thursday and has been doing things like that ever since. He has laid hands upon all the available reading in the house and seems to be going at it six books at a time. Isabel is at work doing some – (The rest of the letter is not to be found.)

In 1891 Wells was able to marry his cousin Isabel. It had been a long and innocent courtship, the magic of which he captured in *Love and Mr. Lewisham*. But as their incompatibility soon became apparent, Wells realized he had made a mistake in his choice of wife. "It was a secretly very embittered young husband," he noted in his autobiography, "who went on catching trains, correcting correspondence answer books, eviscerating rabbits and frogs . . ." In the autumn of 1892 a new student, Catherine Robbins, joined his class. Lively, pretty and bright, she attracted him at once and was, in due course, to become his second wife.

In 1891 Wells married his cousin, the "grave and lovely" Isabel.

Stress at home and overwork brought on another physical collapse. In 1893 Wells began to cough blood as he hurried to Charing Cross to catch his train home. That night he had a massive hemorrhage. He narrowly survived. "I guess class teaching is over for me for good," he wrote to Miss Robbins. "Whether I like it or not, I must write for a living now."

In 1892 Wells met a new student, Catherine Robbins, who later became his second wife.

At Eastbourne in Sussex, where he went to convalesce, he discovered one secret of writing success. In a local library he found a copy of J. M. Barrie's *When a Man's Single*, in which a character claims he can write a salable article about any everyday object: a pipe, a straw, a flower pot. To Wells that idea was an inspiration. He had been writing only for specialist, intellectual markets. Now "all I had to do was to lower my aim – and hit." He scribbled an article called "On Staying at the Seaside" and sent it to the *Pall Mall Gazette*. He received a proof copy by return post, with a demand for more. That was the first of some thirty articles published in 1893. So began Wells's new career in journalism. Within two months he was earning more than ever before.

Most of these articles were intended only to amuse, but the best were more ambitious, explaining to a popular market the possibilities of science. So imaginative are some of these that they became what he himself defined as "the poetry of science." In "The Dream Bureau" he imagines an institution that will create favorite dreams to order. In "The Advent of the Flying Man" he foresees the coming of flight: "the pleasure of such travelling; locomotion free from friction; the earth spread out below, and the sweet air rushing by." "The Man of the Year Million" (1893) describes how man will evolve in the distant future into a new kind of creature:

> There grows upon the impatient imagination a building, a dome of crystal across the translucent surface of which flushes of the most glorious and pure prismatic colours pass and fade and change. In the centre of this transparent chameleon-tinted dome is a circular white marble basin filled with some clear, mobile, amber liquid, and in this plunge and float strange beings. Are they birds?
>
> They are the descendants of man – at dinner. Watch them as they hop on their hands . . . about the pure white marble floor. Great hands they have, enormous brains, soft, liquid, soulful eyes . . .

More somber speculations reflect his study of Darwin. Wells's article "The Extinction of Man" (1894) foresees threats to man's domination of the earth. Like the dinosaurs, man will one day disappear.

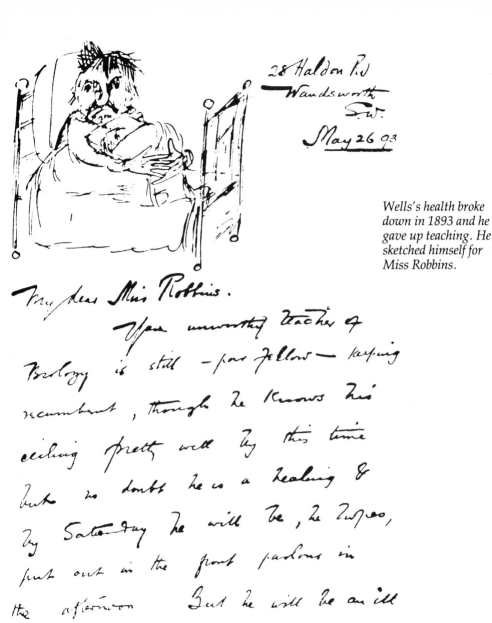

28 Haldon Rd
Wandsworth
S.W.
May 26 03

Wells's health broke
down in 1893 and he
gave up teaching. He
sketched himself for
Miss Robbins.

My dear Miss Robbins,
   Your unworthy teacher of biology is still – poor fellow – keeping
recumbent, though he knows his ceiling pretty well by this time,
but no doubt he is a-healing and by Saturday he will be, he hopes,
put out in the front parlour in the afternoon. But he will be an
ill thing to see, lank and unshaven and with the cares of this world
growing up to choke him as he sprouts out of his bed. However
that is your affair, only you must not make it a matter of mockery.

"The Man of the Year Million" described in an 1893 essay.

We think that we shall always go to work at ten and leave off at five and have dinner at seven for ever and ever ... But even now, for all we can tell, the coming terror may be crouching for its spring and the fall of humanity be at hand.

In the story "The Star" Wells imagines the near destruction of earth when it almost collides with an asteroid from outer space. Here London crowds watch the "star" growing larger in the night sky.

At this time, too, when short stories were an immense vogue, Wells began his distinctive contribution to the genre. "The Stolen Bacillus," "The Flowering of the Strange Orchid" and "The Star" were some of his outstanding pieces based on a "scientific twist." He wrote interestingly about the creative process behind such stories, comparing it to dreaming: "I found that ... there would presently come out of the darkness ... some absurd or vivid little nucleus. Little men in canoes upon sunlit oceans would come floating out of nothingness ... I would discover I was peering into remote and mysterious worlds."

At the end of 1893 came another dramatic change of course in Wells's life: he left his wife, Isabel – "the gently firm champion of all I felt was suppressing me" – to elope with Catherine Robbins. Appeals from all sides left them unmoved. They took rooms near Euston, and Wells began "writing away for dear life" (he also had to support his parents and brothers at this time), breaking off only to walk London streets with Catherine in the hunt for new ideas for articles.

It was a favorable time to begin a writing career. The spread of mass schooling after the 1870 Education Act had created a massive reading public, for both popular and serious works. New technology made printing cheaper and easier. Newspapers, magazines and new publishers hungry for material sprang up in the 1890s as never before. Wells was caught up in this paper tide; he and Catherine were "like two respectable little ordinary shares in a stock exchange boom."

At the end of 1893 Wells left his wife to elope with Catherine Robbins.

The young "Shakespeare of science fiction" who wrote The Time Machine *in 1895.*

In 1894 Wells met W. E. Henley, the poet and editor of *The National Observer*. For him Wells revived his "peculiar treasure," the idea of time travel first drafted as *The Chronic Argonauts*. Seven articles on the subject were published in Henley's paper between March and June. Wells then recast the articles as a serial story. "It is my trump card and if it does not come off I shall know my place for the rest of my career," Wells told a friend.

The Time Machine was published in 1895 and became an instant best-seller. The reading public recognized the book's imaginative power and it became the foundation of Wells's literary fortunes. The influential critic W. T. Stead hailed Wells as "a man of genius."

The story tells of an eccentric inventor, the Time Traveler, who journeys forward in time to the year A.D. 802,701. The final text was one of the most carefully worked of all Wells's novels. Here he abandoned the complicated, self-consciously literary manner of *The Chronic Argonauts* and wrote in the urgent, plain style that was to become his hallmark.

From his favorite book, *Gulliver's Travels* by Jonathan Swift, he borrowed the trick of setting the fantastic

against a prosaic, everyday background. Wells managed to be what his friend, the novelist Joseph Conrad, called "the realist of the fantastic" by using "improbabilities ingeniously made probable." So, when Wells describes his Time Machine ("parts were of nickel, parts of ivory . . . there is an odd twinkling appearance about this bar, as though it was in some way unreal") he is using, as the critic Edward Shanks noticed, "sleight of hand . . . It is almost charlatanry but it is amazingly well done. The surroundings, the incidentals, are made as vivid and real as possible, while nothing definite is said of the object which is really the centre of the picture . . . Mr. Wells gives one or two meaningless details, and our imagination fills in the rest."

The imagined sensations of time travel are described in *The Time Machine* with a poetic intensity unmatched in Wells's other writing. A recent critic has called such passages "the prose equivalent of the great poem of nineteenth-century science the poets of the time never wrote."

> Presently as I went on, still gaining velocity, the palpitation of night and day merged into one continuous greyness; the sky took on a wonderful deepness of blue, a splendid luminous colour like that of early twilight; the jerking sun became a streak of fire, a brilliant arch, in space . . . I saw trees growing and changing like puffs of vapour, now brown, now green; they grew, spread, shivered and passed away. I saw huge buildings rise up faint and fair, and pass away like dreams. The whole surface of the earth seemed changed – melting and flowing under my eyes. The little hands upon the dial that registered my speed raced round faster and faster . . .
>
> (*The Time Machine*, Ch. 3, 1895)

Wells's future world is not the golden age that the Traveler first imagines it to be. It is brutally divided; man has evolved into two species – the gentle, ineffectual Eloi, who live on the surface of the earth, and the savage Morlocks, who live beneath. Wells had described in the extreme the tendencies apparent in his own England, where the rich occupied the best parts of the ground space, pushing the poor away from the sun. ("Even now, does not the East End worker live in such artificial

conditions as practically to be cut off from the natural surface of the earth?") The Morlocks, who use the Eloi as cattle, have all the energy and ingenuity left in the descendants of modern man. The Time Traveler hates them, but, like Gulliver among the Yahoos, he cannot help identifying with them. ("I'm starving for a bit of meat.")

Wells's story is deeply pessimistic. From his studies of Darwinism under Huxley, he drew the idea that evolution could run backward, that man could revert to an animal state and fall into decline. He therefore argues against the widely held Victorian faith in progress, which assumed that humankind would continue to improve and become more powerful, more sophisticated, more intelligent. As the Time Traveler walks around the great Museum of Man, he realizes that "the

Opposite Wells's subterranean Morlocks were his projection of the poor working class of his own day.

A Punch cartoon satirizing Darwin's theory of evolution. Wells took this theory into the future in The Time Machine, *showing how humankind would evolve, decay and disappear.*

growing pile of civilization [is] only a foolish heaping that must inevitably fall back upon and destroy its makers in the end." Here Wells reflects the characteristic *fin de siècle* mood of the 1890s and his reading of theories, such as those of Max Nordau, that nineteenth-century civilization was in decay and man himself degenerating.

The magnificent "Further Vision" that concludes *The Time Machine* is perhaps the finest thing Wells ever wrote. The Traveler goes on in time to see the end of the world. As the sun burns out, the last living things retreat into the sea.

> So I travelled ... in great strides of a thousand years or more, drawn on by the mystery of the earth's fate, watching with a strange fascination the sun grow larger and duller in the westward sky, and the life of the old earth ebb away. At last, more than thirty million years hence, the huge red-hot dome of the sun had come to obscure nearly a tenth part of the darkling heavens ... I saw nothing moving, in earth or sky or sea. The green slime on the rocks alone testified that life was not extinct. A shallow sand bank had appeared in the sea ... I fancied I saw some black object flopping about upon this bank ... It was a round thing, the size of a football perhaps ... and tentacles trailed down from it; it seemed black against the weltering blood-red water, and it was hopping fitfully about ...

A *Daily Chronicle* reviewer noted that "the description of the sea-coast of the dying ocean still embracing a dying world, and of the huge hideous creeping thing which are the last remains of life on our worn-out planet has real impressiveness – it grips the imagination as it is only gripped by the genuinely imaginative." Wells echoes, and colors with his scientific contemplations, a favorite theme of earlier nineteenth-century Romantic writers – the Last Man. His Time Traveler is like the poet Thomas Campbell's solitary survivor:

> The sun had a sickly glare;
> The earth with age was wan;
> The skeletons of the nations were
> Around that lonely man.

> (Thomas Campbell, "The Last Man," 1842)

3 The Shakespeare of Science Fiction

By the end of 1895 Wells had begun to make his name as a writer. Collections of his essays, short stories and a novel, *The Wonderful Visit* (in which an angel appears in an English village), were published to support the reputation won by *The Time Machine*. *The Island of Dr. Moreau* was about to appear. This is a grim fable about a scientist who uses surgery to transform animals into hideous human-like creatures. "It's rather pleasant to find oneself something in the world after all the years of trying and disappointment," Wells wrote to his mother in October.

In the same month he married Catherine and they settled in a house in Woking, Surrey. Here mornings were devoted to work; afternoons to walks or cycling in the nearby countryside. Wells became an avid cyclist,

Wells and his wife became avid cyclists: both The Wheels of Chance *and* Mr. Polly *reflect this interest.*

and, on a tandem specially designed for him, took his wife on long rides. His charming comedy *The Wheels of Chance* (1896) was a product of this enthusiasm for cycling.

An illustration from The War of the Worlds, *in its first magazine publication. The octopus-like Martians and these tripod fighting machines begin the conquest of earth.*

Wells also used his bicycle to collect local color for his next "scientific romance," *The War of the Worlds* (1898), which describes a Martian invasion of earth. Wells said his book was inspired by a remark made by his brother Frank as they walked across the Surrey heathland: "Suppose some beings from another planet were to drop out of the sky suddenly and begin laying

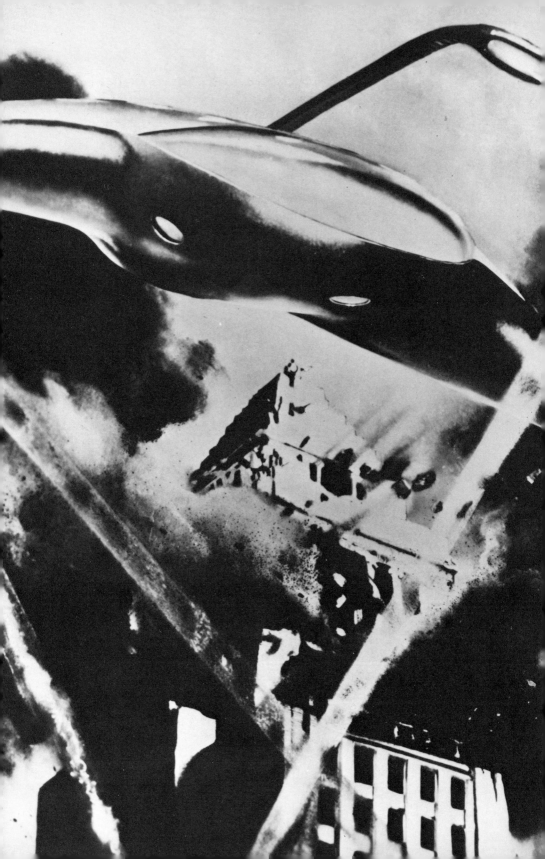

about them here." Mars was in the news in the 1890s; a light had been seen on the planet and a pattern of "canals" supposedly traced. Wells's Martians, escaping their dying planet, travel to earth in huge, cylindrical spacecraft. Several land in Surrey, and after devastating the district with their laser-like "Heat Ray" and poisonous "Black Smoke," the Martians attack and easily conquer London. Although sluggish, octopus-shaped creatures themselves, their advanced technology has created massive tripod fighting machines in which they are nearly invincible:

> And this Thing I saw! How can I describe it? A monstrous tripod, higher than many houses, striding over the young pine trees and smashing them aside in its career; a walking engine of glittering metal . . . Machine it was, with a ringing metallic pace, and long, flexible, glittering tentacles (one of which gripped a young pine tree) swinging and rattling about its strange body . . . The brazen hood that surmounted it moved to and fro with the inevitable suggestion of a head looking about it . . . Puffs of green smoke squirted out from the joints of the limbs as the monster swept by me . . . As it passed it set up an exultant deafening howl that drowned the thunder – "Aloo! Aloo!"

(The War of the Worlds, Ch. 10)

Wells was writing within a special genre – the invasion story – made popular by Sir George Chesney's *Battle of Dorking* (1871), in which Britain is invaded by Prussia. Many variations of this theme were published during the late Victorian era, mostly intended as a warning against British Imperial complacency. Wells's book was a clever variation of the idea – the enemy is from outer space. One feature of the invasion story was its careful description of the topography to give the narrative conviction. Wells used the same device. He recalled later how he used to "take his bicycle of an afternoon and note the houses and cottages and typical inhabitants to be destroyed after tea by the Heat Ray, or smothered in the Red Weed." The everyday detail of the London suburbs ravaged by the Martians adds conviction to the fantastic Martians; it is his familiar method of "domesticating the impossible."

The War of the Worlds also reveals Wells's delight in

fantasies of violence and destruction that he had indulged in since boyhood. Violence is a constant motif in his work; most of his early books contain a destructive fire. In his picture of hysterical crowds leaving London, Wells borrowed from a favorite source: Daniel Defoe's *Journal of the Plague Year* (1722), which recorded another panic exodus from the city in 1665. Wells also uncannily anticipated the August 1914 newspaper descriptions of Belgian refugees fleeing from the advancing Germans. His understanding of crowd hysteria was truly impressive. It was demonstrated by a remarkable radio version of *The War of the Worlds* broadcast in the United States

Opposite *The British Army's feeble artillery of 1898 is easily destroyed by the Martians.*

In 1938 Orson Welles's radio version of The War of the Worlds *caused widespread panic in the United States.*

THE EVENING SUN

BALTIMORE, MONDAY, OCTOBER 31, 1938

DIO SCARE BRINGS U. S. PROBE

ORSON WELLES

ALL-AMERICAN BOGEYMAN

in 1938. Orson Welles, the famous movie director, recast the story as a news program announcing the landing of Martians in New Jersey. Panic spread among listeners, and thousands fled their homes. Psychologists who later studied the phenomenon noted how the program had revealed deep-seated fears and insecurities in the audience. Wells, too, had played on the fears of his Victorian readers. (The text of the broadcast is given in *The Invasion from Mars* by Hadley Cantrill, 1940.)

Wells's story, like several of his other works, can be seen as a myth with many messages and themes. There is its anticolonial theme. Just as Europeans had suddenly invaded and destroyed the lifestyles of simpler peoples in Africa and Australia, so the Martians invade and destroy us:

> The Tasmanians, in spite of their human likeness, were entirely swept out of existence in a war of extermination waged by European immigrants, in the space of fifty years. Are we such apostles of mercy as to complain if the Martians warred in the same spirit?

> (*The War of the Worlds*, Ch. 1)

Wells extends this idea to man's treatment of other creatures. Before we judge the Martians too harshly "we must remember what ruthless and utter destruction our own species has wrought upon animals, such as the vanished bison and dodo." Thus his story expresses a concern for wildlife conservation that is still relevant today.

But the major theme of *The War of the Worlds*, and one that dominates many of Wells's early essays, is that humankind had become over confident about the future. "But even now the coming terror may be crouching for its spring and the fall of humanity be at hand."

Wells uses his biological background to provide the brilliant, ironic twist that forms the novel's climax. The super-powerful Martians are destroyed by the humblest living things on earth: the bacteria. An early critic noted the power of this episode: "The picture of the last Martian, in its bewildered agony, howling in the twilight from the summit of Primrose Hill over a silent and devastated London, is one of the most effective which we have met for many years. We shall long hear 'Ulla! Ulla!' echoing in our dreams."

Opposite *Panic-stricken crowds try to escape the Martians: some people have been set on fire by the "Heat Ray."*

The mad scientist, Griffin, who makes himself invisible so that he can wage war against society.

The Invisible Man (1897) was another product of Wells's time at Woking. Griffin, an insane scientist, invents a way of making himself invisible. He plans to use his power to terrorize society. The description of Griffin's first experience of becoming invisible clearly demonstrates Wells's astonishing imagination.

I shall never forget that dawn, and the strange horror of seeing my hands had become as clouded glass, and watching them grow clearer and thinner as the day went by ... My limbs became glassy, the bones and arteries faded, vanished, and the little white nerves went last ... At last only the dead tips of the finger nails remained, pallid and white, and the brown stain of some acid upon my fingers ... I went and stared at nothing in my shaving-glass – at nothing, save merely an attenuated pigment still remained behind the retina of my eyes, fainter than mist ...

(*The Invisible Man*, Ch. 20)

Wells engaged a literary agent, James Pinker, to promote his books. This was an uncommon practice at that time, but it helped to enhance Wells's reputation. His books were very successful abroad and were soon translated into many languages. He told his brother: "People I have never seen, some from Chicago, one from Cape Town, and one from far up the Yang Tse Kiang in China, write to me and tell me they find my books pleasant." Wells had become one of the first of the modern international authors. A fellow novelist, Ford Madox Ford, remembered the first impact of the scientific romances: "Here was genius ... Fairy tales are a prime necessity of the world and he and science were going to provide us with a perfectly new brand. And he did ... And all great London lay prostrate at his feet." If Edgar Alan Poe and Jules Verne came before him, the originality of his themes – space invasion, time travel, catastrophe, alien worlds – make Wells the first great science-fiction writer. A recent leading writer in the field, Brian Aldiss, has called Wells "the Prospero of all the brave new worlds of the mind, and the Shakespeare of science fiction."

Wells and his wife moved to a still bigger house in Worcester Park – another stage in Wells's life-long quest for the perfect working place – and began to mix in London literary society. With his high-pitched voice and cockney accent, Wells was at first shy and uneasy. Dorothy Richardson, a writer friend, observed the couple's "curious hard emptiness like people rehearsing." Yet she also saw Wells's enormous charm and the fascination of his conversation. For him this was a time of new friendships. He became close to George Gissing,

52

a novelist who was as relentless a failure as Wells was a success. He corresponded with Joseph Conrad, the Polish sea captain turned writer, whose books Wells had been one of the first to praise in review. Wells's special confidant was Arnold Bennett, whose struggle to success had been something like his own.

The furious pace of his writing slowed in 1898 when illness overcame him again. After a long struggle to finish *When the Sleeper Wakes* and *Love and Mr. Lewisham*, he took a south coast cycling vacation, only to collapse on the way. While recovering at Sandgate in Kent, he found he liked its climate and decided to have a house built on the cliffs. C. F. A. Voysey, a fashionable architect, was commissioned to design what Wells called "Spade House."

When the Sleeper Wakes (1899), one of Wells's "fantasias of possibility," is more laboriously written than the other

Opposite *Wells imagined many aspects of future technology, including aircraft, in* When the Sleeper Wakes.

Below *In* When the Sleeper Wakes *a Victorian Englishman falls asleep, waking 200 years later. Here he looks down on the vast domed city of the future with its moving roadways.*

scientific romances, yet it does display the author's much-praised gift for predicting the future. A Victorian Englishman falls into a deep trance, waking two hundred years later. Civilization has retreated into the "super city" or "megalopolis" – London consists of towering buildings covered with a glass dome. Society is ruthlessly divided. The rich and powerful live high up near the light; the working masses toil in the "glaring labyrinth" below. It is a harsh picture designed as an antidote to more optimistic nineteenth-century projections of the future, such as Edward Bellamy's *Looking Backward* (1888) or William Morris's *News from Nowhere* (1891). If the story is dull, the mechanical predictions are intriguing – the moving roadways, the videotape machines, the air service to Paris.

A Story of the Days to Come (1899) is a brief fiction using the same mega-city background. Two young people decide to escape from the great city to live a simpler, more natural life in the empty countryside outside. This is a seminal story in the science fiction genre. The theme of the individual in revolt against an oppressive, machine-dominated society was taken up in E. M. Forster's *The Machine Stops* (1909) and in Yevgeny Zamiatin's Russian novel *We* (1924), which in turn inspired Aldous Huxley's *Brave New World* (1932) and George Orwell's *Nineteen Eighty-Four* (1948).

The First Men in the Moon (1901) is Wells's last important scientific romance. He borrowed from the long tradition of the "super terrestrial voyage" story, which stretched from the Roman writer Lucian to the fiction of Jules Verne. He also drew on the latest scientific papers in creating his own lunar journey, imagined sixty-nine years before men actually stepped onto the moon. His travelers, Bedford and Cavor, cross space in a sphere coated with antigravity material. Wells's moon is hollow and contains an advanced civilization of Selenites (moon-dwellers) led by the mighty brain, the Grand Lunar. The swiftly moving story contains some of Wells's most haunting creative description. The lunar sunrise that melts the frozen air and covers the surface with fantastic vegetation has been admired by the twentieth-century poet T. S. Eliot as "absolutely unforgettable."

54

Out of the gullies and flats that had been hidden from us but not from the quickening sun . . . a bristling beard of spiky and fleshy vegetation was straining into view . . . It was like a miracle that growth. So, one must imagine, the trees and plants arose at the Creation, and covered the desolation of the new-made earth.

Imagine it! Imagine that dawn! The resurrection of the frozen air, the stirring and quickening of the soil, and then this silent uprising of vegetation . . .

(The First Men in the Moon, Ch. 8)

If the influence of Wells's favorite, *Gulliver's Travels*, is apparent in the conversations between Cavor and the Grand Lunar (which are very like those between Gulliver and the King of Brobdingnag), it is even clearer in *The Food of the Gods* (1904), in which a scientist invents a substance that makes living things grow larger. He is careless with it, and southern England is soon infested with giant rats, wasps, hideous pond creatures, thistles and fungi. Then the Food is given to human babies . . .

Although there were important themes in the scientific romances, Wells consciously turned away from the genre after 1900. Sometimes the imaginative magic returned: in *The War in the Air* (1908) and *The World Set Free* (1914), and in certain short stories, such as "Brownlow's Newspaper" (1932) in which a man in 1931 receives an evening paper from 1971, which gives him fascinating glimpses of the world's future.

Opposite *Cavor and Bedford come face to face with moon creatures, the Selenites of* The First Men in the Moon.

The Selenite ruling class are huge brains, whose bodies are so feeble that these "wobbling jellies of knowledge" have to be carried everywhere.

4
Considering Society

Wells and his young family at Spade House, Sandgate, Kent. The house, which was specially designed for him, symbolized his success as a writer.

Spade House was Wells's home for his next triumphant decade. It was a light, spacious dwelling, with a glorious garden sloping to the cliff edge, and symbolized the author's escape from the underground kitchens and servants' quarters in which he began life. In his "treasure house by the sea," Wells built up his health and wrote some of his best-known books. Here his two sons were born. "Wells is a happy man – how he flourishes," commented a friend.

The house was always open to visitors. Impatient with the formalities of Edwardian entertainment, Wells devised his own style, which involved active games, especially charades, or a miniature war game played with model soldiers (the rules were set out in his book *Little Wars* (1931)). One visitor, the social critic C. F. G. Masterman, recalled "an impression of perpetual sunshine, health and ease."

Catherine (or Jane, as her husband called her) worked tirelessly to help Wells's work, arranging translations, reading proofs, handling business. She also had to endure the darker side of Wells's personality, his black moods that found domestic life claustrophobic and drove him away from home for weeks at a time. His first biographer, Geoffrey West, declared that "his soul has a side scarcely less concealed and strange than that of the moon."

Wells took seriously the games he played with his sons. They developed into elaborate war games like this, which he described in Little Wars *(1913).*

Wells enjoyed a new kind of success with *Anticipations* (1901), a series of essays about life in the dawning twentieth century that provided a "rough sketch of the coming time." At the turn of the century futurology was in fashion, and Wells's book was as popular as a bestselling novel. He began with predictions of highways and wars fought with aircraft and concluded with a plan for a "New Republic," a World State that would eventually evolve, based on the "higher sanity" of humankind.

Anticipations won the admiration of Beatrice and Sidney Webb, who had helped to form the Fabian Society.

The Fabian Society, which Wells joined in 1903, was a group of middle-class socialists, who pioneered many features of the Welfare State. Leading members were Bernard Shaw, Beatrice and Sidney Webb and Graham Wallas.

The Fabians were middle-class socialists who believed in the reconstruction of society by well-considered reform rather than by sudden revolution. Their work was the basis of the modern Welfare State. Beatrice thought that Wells would be "a good instrument for popularizing ideas." Wells began to attend her London dinner parties, where he met some of the leading figures of the time. He was amazed at the way his books had transformed his life. "Writing is a form of adventure," he commented later. "If your book has the least bit of luck you become a prosperous man. Suddenly you are able to go where you like, meet whoever you like. All

BERTHA NEWCOMBE

61

doors are open to you. One sees the world. One meets the rich and the great . . . One finds oneself hearing and touching at first hand the big discussions that sway men."

Wells joined the Fabian Society, seeing it at first as made up of the élite who would create his New Republic. He was soon disillusioned. In any case he was too individual, too little used to working with others. His attempts, in 1906, to enlarge the Society and make its propaganda more dramatic caused much irritation, which he belittled as "a storm in a Fabian teacup." Wells consoled himself by resigning in 1908 and by writing mocking portraits of the Webbs as "prigs at play" in his novel *The New Machiavelli* (1911).

In The Food of the Gods *a scientist invents a substance that makes living things bigger. Here giant rats threaten the Kent countryside.*

Max Beerbohm's cartoon attacks Wells's version of the future as shown in his A Modern Utopia *(1905).*

Meanwhile, in 1905, the year he published *A Modern Utopia*, an imaginative picture of an ideal society, and his social novel *Kipps*, Wells was at the height of his reputation. "I am lost in amazement at the diversity of your genius," wrote the great novelist Henry James in a letter to Wells.

Wells was ambitious to prove himself a "serious" novelist. When Arnold Bennett protested against his abandoning the "scientific romance," Wells answered "Why the Hell have you joined the conspiracy to restrain me to one type of story? I want to write novels and before God I will write novels." As fiction critic for the *Saturday Review* in the mid-1890s, Wells had concluded that the novel was "the most vital and typical art of the country and period." He particularly admired writers such as Thomas Hardy (*Jude the Obscure* was his favorite), Gissing and Conrad whose work depicted

Wells continued to be a brilliant and original short story writer. This is a scene from "The Man Who Could Work Miracles."

individual lives that reflected the great social forces of their time. Wells's successful novels of the first decade of the century – *Love and Mr. Lewisham, Kipps, Tono-Bungay* and *The History of Mr. Polly* – were in this style. Their enduring force comes, however, from their autobiographical themes. These early heroes (his "Little Men") were, he said, victims of "perplexity, frustration, humiliation and waste of energy ... the common lot of human beings in a phase of blindly changing human conditions." But, like Wells himself, they escape, in various ways, from the traps in which they find themselves. Through the characters of Kipps and Ponderevo (in *Tono-Bungay*), whose sudden wealth brings a rise in social status, Wells explores the changes and confusion brought to his own life by writing success.

Kipps tells the story of a draper's assistant whose life is transformed when he inherits a fortune. Wealth does not give happiness; Kipps escapes from the wretched life of the shop to find himself trapped again in the "respectable" conventions of life among the wealthy. The published novel is only a fragment of a much longer

In the picture of Shalford's Drapery Bazaar in Kipps, Wells looked back angrily to his own days in the draper's trade.

projected work, called "The Wealth of Mr. Waddy," begun in 1898; this had been intended as a "complete study of life in relation to England's social condition," composed in the old Victorian three-volume format. Changes in publishing conditions made the scale of the book uneconomic, and only its central section, the story of Kipps himself, went into print (although the opening section about Mr. Waddy, Kipps's benefactor, did survive and was published in 1969).

The book begins with some semi-autobiographical episodes about Kipps's childhood and schooling, his romance with Anne – they cut a sixpence in two as a love token – and his apprenticeship at Shalford's Drapery Bazaar. These passages are some of Wells's best writing; they inspired Henry James, a stern critic, to describe the novel as "vivid, sharp and raw." The succeeding sections are less satisfactory; the freshness disappears and Wells's sociological views take over. The grim commentaries of the socialist Masterman (partly based on the novelist George Gissing) and the comments of the outside narrator seem intrusive and out of scale. The novel is an uneasy reflection of Wells's changing styles and interests during the seven years he took to complete it. Yet there are episodes – the "anagram tea," Kipps's embarrassed dinner at the Royal Grand Hotel – that show Wells's humor and satire at their sharpest.

C. F. G. Masterman saw *Kipps* as an important document of Edwardian life, and its hero as "a figure of ultimate significance . . . the shallow, unsatisfied, awkward product of city civilization."

> The stupid little tragedies of these clipped and limited lives! Above them, brooding over them, I tell you there is a monster, like some great, clumsy griffin thing . . . like pride, like indolence, like all that is darkening and heavy and obstructive in life . . . It is the ruling power of this land, Stupidity . . . I see through the darkness the souls of Mr. Kippses as they are, as little pinkish strips of quivering, living stuff . . . And the claw of this Beast rests upon them.
>
> (*Kipps*, Book 3, Ch. 2)

Tono-Bungay is perhaps Wells's most impressive novel. In this story of Edward Ponderevo, whose

Wells's own drawing of his "little man" hero, Arthur Kipps.

invention of a patent medicine brings him an immense fortune, Wells satirizes the restlessness and vulgarity of Edwardian Britain: "forces turning to waste . . . people who use and do not replace . . . a country hectic with a wasting, aimless fever of trade and money-making and pleasure seeking!" Wells's main theme is aimless greed. Ponderevo pours his ill-gotten fortune into a massive country mansion, Crest Hill, whose extravagances were taken from actual building projects of the Edwardian "super-rich."

He moved a quite considerable hill, and nearly sixty mature trees were moved with it to open his prospect eastward ... At another time he caught a suggestion from some city restaurant and made a billiard room roofed with plate glass beneath the water of his ornamental lake. He furnished one wing while its roof still awaited completion. He had a swimming bath thirty feet square next to his bedroom upstairs, and to crown it all he commenced a great wall to hold his dominions together ... It was a ten foot wall ... and it would have had a total length of nearly eleven miles ...

It is curious how many of these modern financiers of chance and bluff have ended their careers by building ... Sooner or later they all seem to bring their luck to the test of realization ... bring moonshine in relations with a weekly wages sheet. Then the whole fabric of confidence and imagination totters – and down they come.

Tono-Bungay
attacked the wasteful, empty lives of the Edwardian "super rich."

(*Tono-Bungay*, Book 3, Ch. 10)

The History of Mr. Polly (1910) is memorable for its charm and comedy. Wells called it his happiest book, written in a mood "in which he felt he could go on writing for ever." It has a unity unusual in Wells's novels, and a sharp satirical edge. Polly is a daydreaming social misfit, who escapes a loveless marriage and frustrated life as a draper by running away to become a tramp. Wells's own father and his brother Frank (who gave up drapery to become an itinerant clock-mender) are the models for Polly. Wells resented the waste in their lives, that they were "netted in greyness and discomfort – with life dancing all about." He was angry that "in a social order where all good things go to those who watch, grab and clutch . . . the quality of my father, the rich humour and imagination of my brother Frank were shoved out of play and wasted altogether."

Beneath the humor, *The History of Mr. Polly* is an angry book, criticizing a society that "accumulates useless and aimless lives, as a man accumulates fat and morbid products in his blood." A reviewer noted this theme of "huge and pitiless waste" in a system that "lavishly produces the 'little man' and yet seems to provide no place for him. He wedges himself into it only to be ruthlessly

Mr. Polly's comic battle with Uncle Jim is a fight for his own identity and self-respect: a scene from the 1949 movie version of The History of Mr. Polly.

squeezed out."

Against this unsatisfactory city way of life, Wells sets a daydream life of the English countryside. As in *The Wheels of Chance*, Wells creates a radiant vision of rural England before the automobile destroyed its peace: "footpaths haphazard across fields . . . unknown winding lanes between high hedges of honeysuckle and dog rose . . . green bridle-paths through primrose-studded undergrowths . . . pools and ponds and shining threads of rivers . . . flower-starred hedgerows." Wells echoes the nostalgia of other writers of the time – the poet Edward Thomas and Kenneth Grahame, author of *The Wind in the Willows* (1908) – for the rural world as an escape from industrialism and the city. Polly escapes to find happiness and a real identity in the countryside of the Potwell Inn: "It was as if everything lay securely within a great warm friendly globe of crystal sky. It was as safe and enclosed and fearless as a child that has still to be born." Wells's vision was sentimental. His friend Charles Masterman wrote, in *The Condition of England* (1909), a scathing attack on the poverty and degradation of the real rural England that was still in the grip of a severe agricultural depression.

Polly is a victim of social injustice who changes his life by determined action, thus following Wells's own maxim: "If the world does not please you, you can change it." Humiliated by poor education, by commercialism, by the institution of marriage, Polly is trapped. On the eve of his "suicide," he reflects:

> And this was the end of life for him! The end! And it seemed to him now that life had never begun for him, never! It was as if his soul had been cramped and his eyes bandaged from the hour of his birth. Why had he lived such a life? Why had he submitted to things, blundered into things? Why had he never insisted on the things he thought beautiful and the things he desired . . . They were the things that mattered . . . A living did not matter unless there were things to live for . . .
>
> (*The History of Mr. Polly*, Ch. 8)

Opposite Wells's late Victorian and Edwardian social novels give delightful glimpses of the old English countryside before the coming of the automobile.

Then he takes action and begins to live positively. His fight against "Uncle Jim," comic though it is, is his battle to find self-respect.

The brilliantly described minor characters – Uncle Penstemon, the rebel apprentice Parsons, Polly's wife Miriam, his fellow shopkeepers, Uncle Jim – are vivid enough to justify the contemporary claims that Wells was a second Dickens. The set pieces, such as Polly's wedding or his father's funeral, are also Dickensian. An early reviewer noted of these sketches of lower middle-class life that "a whole section of English society makes its first appearance in English literature . . . just as they are, in their marriages and funerals."

Wells's final collection of stories appeared in 1911. He tended to make light of his work as mere entertainment, yet the critic Edward Shanks, in a penetrating comment, saw in the best of the stories a poetic imagination that was Wells's greatest gift as a writer: "They are, in their degree, myths; and Mr. Wells is a myth-maker."

"The Country of the Blind" (1912) is one of his most fascinating tales. A man crosses a remote mountain range to discover a valley where nobody has eyes. He thinks a sighted man will easily come to dominate these people. Instead he is mocked and controlled by them. Wells, perhaps, felt this was an image of his own condition as an isolated man of genius born into an intolerant, narrow-minded world that rejected his ideas.

"The Door in the Wall" (1906), another haunting tale, was picked out by Shanks as "among the half dozen or so things which, I believe, constitute his permanent contribution to English literature." A boy enters a beautiful and mysterious garden through a door in its wall. As he grows up, he longs to re-enter the garden, but, although he sometimes sees the door, he can never find the chance to enter it. The story has many possible meanings. A recent critic has seen the garden as a personal symbol of Wells's first youthful imaginative gift that he could never recapture in middle age.

After 1911 Wells wrote many more novels, but his early inspiration deserted him. In his letters to the novelist Henry James, Wells theorized at length about the novel as an instrument of social reform. It was to be "the vehicle of understanding, the parade of morals . . . the factory of customs, the criticism of laws and institutions, and of social dogmas and ideas . . . Before we have done, we will have all life within the scope of the novel." Yet the more Wells theorized, the less interesting his

Opposite *"The Country of the Blind" is one of Wells's greatest symbolic short stories. Here the sighted Nunez, who has discovered the secret country, is examined by the eyeless inhabitants.*

Ann Veronica *was a controversial novel because it discussed the status of women in society at the time of the suffragette protests.*

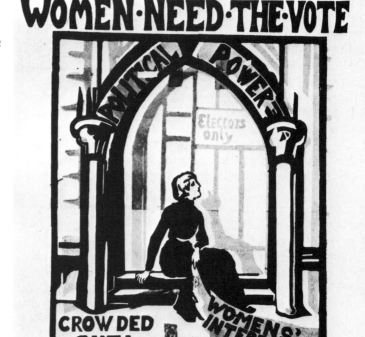

own novels became.

Moreover, scandal about his writing began to make Wells many enemies. *Ann Veronica* (1909) caused controversy. It is the story of a girl who revolts against the constraints of her middle-class background and joins the suffragettes in their fierce campaign to win votes for women. Then she elopes with a young scientist. The *Spectator* critic led the attack against "this poisonous book," which should, he felt, be banned from libraries. This "literary filth" showed "the muddy world of Mr. Wells's imaginings . . . a community of scuffling stoats and ferrets." For a time Wells's literary and social standing seemed in danger. "I feel as though I was living in a stuffy, slovenly room full of noisy and violent people," he said in a 1911 interview. "All sorts of storms,

boycotts, censorship and foolishness prevent me opening the windows and letting in a little air." However,
the outcry against him only increased his sales. And
to the young, he became a symbol of protest, against
all that is "hateful and hostile to youth and tomorrow."
He loved to lecture to young people, who found him
refreshing and exciting. A particular admirer, the writer
Rebecca West, recalled how "one had the luck to be
young just as the most bubbling, creative mind appeared
that the sun and moon have shone upon since the days
of Leonardo da Vinci." In his work she said, "one could
see the forces of the age sweep and surge."

*The important
feminist writer
Rebecca West was a
close friend and
admirer of Wells.*

In 1912 Wells moved his family to a new home, Easton Glebe, near Dunmow in Essex. The house was enlarged; its gardens laid out by Catherine; its barn converted into a games and dancing room. The life of that house – its summer meals under the trees, its amateur theatricals, its strenuous games of field hockey and handball – are caught in the sunlit opening pages of *Mr. Britling Sees It Through* (1916). There, too, Wells described himself in early middle age:

Easton Glebe in Essex, where Wells and his family moved in 1912.

He loved to write and talk. He talked about everything, he had ideas about everything, he could no more help having ideas about everything than a dog can resist smelling at your heels . . . lots of people found him interesting and stimulating, a few found him seriously exasperating. He had ideas in the utmost profusion . . .

5 Educator and Open Conspirator

In his science fiction Wells had sketched many fantasy wars. *In the Days of the Comet* (1906) sees Europe saved from war only by the arrival of a mysterious comet that alters the human mind by changing the content of earth's atmosphere as it strikes our planet. In *The War in the*

The War in the Air
(1908) describes future world conflict involving aircraft. The hero, Bert Smallways, makes his way across a ruined and chaotic English countryside.

Air (1908), which opens with a German airship raid that destroys New York, conflict brings social collapse:

> Anyone dropped suddenly into the country . . . would have remarked first, perhaps, that all the hedges needed clipping, that the roadside grass grew rank . . . And then suddenly would come the Dureresque element; the skeleton of a horse, or some crumpled mass of rags in the ditch, with gaunt, extended feet and a yellow, purple-blotched skin and face, or what had been a face, gaunt and glaring and devastated. Then here would be a field that had been ploughed and not sown, and here a field of corn carelessly trampled by beasts, and here a hoarding torn down across the road to make a fire. Then presently he would meet a man or a woman, yellow-faced and probably negligently dressed and armed – prowling for food.

> *(The War in the Air, Ch. 10)*

Even more remarkable is *The World Set Free* (1914). Its prediction of the Great War's actual Western Front is striking enough: "From Holland to the Alps this day there must be crouching and lying between half a million and a million of men, trying to inflict irreparable damage upon one another . . ." Wells went further. Working from hints he had heard of the work of the scientists Albert Einstein and Ernest Rutherford, he foresaw man's

Wells just before World War I (1914 to 1918).

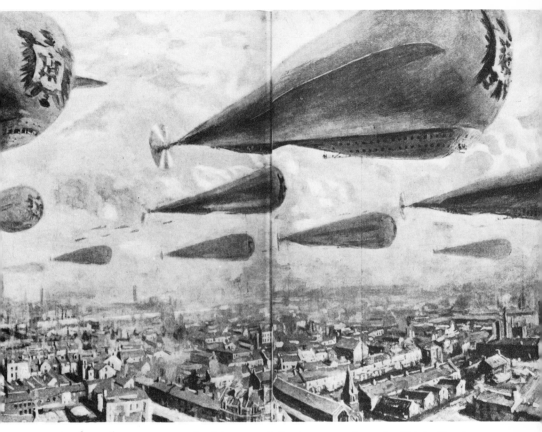

conquest of nuclear energy. In his novel that power is used in atomic bombs (a term added to the language by Wells). Once exploded, Wells's atomic bombs continue to burn forever, like miniature suns. Here French airmen drop them on Berlin:

An illustration from The War in the Air, *showing the German imperial airship fleet crossing England on its way to bomb New York.*

It was like looking down upon the crater of a small volcano. In the open garden before the Imperial Palace a shuddering star of evil splendour spirted and poured up smoke and flame towards them like an accusation. They were too high to distinguish people clearly, or mark the bomb's effect upon the building until suddenly the facade tottered and crumbled in the flare as sugar dissolves in water. The man stared for a moment, showed all his long teeth, and then staggered into the cramped standing position his straps permitted, hoisted out and bit another bomb and set it down after its fellow.

(*The World Set Free*, Ch. 2)

Yet, when World War I actually began in August 1914, Wells was surprised. The declaration was like "the shock of an unexpected big gun fired suddenly within a hundred yards." He had always thought of such a war as a final breakdown into chaos from which would emerge a saner world with perpetual peace. In this spirit he wrote an article, "The war that will end war," the title of which became a catch-phrase and a real inspiration to many British soldiers. "Every sword drawn against Germany now is a sword drawn for peace," he declared. "This war must end war."

By 1915, following the moods of the moment, he moved from this first idealism to produce "shrill jets of journalism" that reflected the current hysterical hatred for Germany and the Kaiser. Finally, like so many

Wells's first enthusiasm for war in 1914 soon changed to disillusion. This is an antiwar cartoon by Louis Raemaeker called "The harvest is ripe."

others, he became disillusioned, finding, by 1916, that "We were being ordered about in the King's war with Germany." His shifting moods are recorded in the best-selling war novel, *Mr. Britling Sees It Through*.

Visits to the trench lines increased his pessimism. War was being waged with outdated methods. He contrasted the old-fashioned officer class, "fine, handsome, well-groomed, neighing gentlemen," with the real war-winners, the men of science working on new weapons, "with our bits of stick and iron pipe and wire, our test-tubes and our incalculable possibilities." (In his story "The Land Ironclads" (1903), Wells had predicted the 1916 British invention, the tank.)

In his story "The Land Ironclads" (1903) Wells had foretold the invention of the tank. This 1916 drawing shows how people imagined the tanks might look when they first appeared on the Western Front.

Wells knew the anti-
war poet Siegfried
Sassoon, and agreed
with his bitter attacks
on the conduct of the
war, expressed in
such poems as "The
General."

THE GENERAL.

'Good-morning; good-morning!' the General said
When we met him last week on our way to the Line.
Now the soldiers he smiled at are most of 'em dead,
And we're cursing his staff for incompetent swine.
'He's a cheery old card', grunted Harry to Jack
As they slogged up to Arras with rifle and pack.

         *   *   *

But he did for them both by his plan of attack.

In the later war years Wells campaigned for the proposed "League of Free Nations." For humankind to unite was the only way to end war. In 1918 he joined Lord Northcliffe's Ministry of Propaganda to compose literature for use against Germany.

Wells's final thoughts on the tragedy of the Great War were seen in his comments on the war poet Siegfried Sassoon.

> His song is a cry of anger at the old men who have led the world to destruction. Youth turns upon age, upon laws and institutions, upon the whole elaborate rottenness of the European system, saying, "What is this to which you have brought us? What have you done with our lives?"

> (*Joan and Peter*, Ch. 13, 1918)

Wells's fame was at its height in the 1920s. He was a popular celebrity, a "star," not unlike his friend of that time, the movie comedian Charlie Chaplin. People clapped for him or turned around to stare as he walked down the street. As a journalist he reached a pinnacle of success in 1921 when he received an immense fee to cover the Washington Disarmament Conference; his articles on the conference were syndicated throughout the world. "No journalist had ever before addressed so large an audience," wrote the critic Edward Shanks. He went on to praise Wells's vivid, clear writing style: "He is a spell-binder, a silver tongue."

In the 1920s Wells enjoyed a world fame very like that of his friend, the comic movie star Charlie Chaplin.

In the restless postwar years, Wells began a self-appointed mission to create a united world. This vast, ambitious, and finally fruitless, campaign occupied him for the rest of his life.

The
OUTLINE of HISTORY
BY
H. G. WELLS.

A PLAIN HISTORY OF
LIFE AND MANKIND

Book 1
The Making of
Our World

In his work with the League of Nations Association he had often been surprised at his colleagues' historical ignorance – an ignorance that made discussion difficult. No sound plans for the world's future could be proposed until its past was fully understood. Accordingly, Wells began his epic *The Outline of History*, a record of the progress of humanity from its prehistoric dawn to its exhaustion at the end of World War I. He took a year to research and write this formidable work. He employed a "cyclical" view of history, tracing the rise and fall of nations and empires according to the rise and fall of a creative élite within them. The final message was that the modern world must listen to its own élite or drift into final destruction. Life was now "a race between education and catastrophe." *The Outline of History*, which appeared first as a part-work in 1919, was hailed as a magnificent achievement. It sold millions of copies worldwide, making him richer than ever.

> Life begins perpetually. Gathered together at last under the leadership of man ... unified, disciplined, armed with the secret power of the atom and with knowledge as yet beyond dreaming, Life, for ever dying to be born afresh, for ever young and eager, will presently stand upon this earth as upon a footstool, and stretch out its realm amidst the stars.

(*The Outline of History*, Conclusion, 1919)

During the next decade Wells added two other works to his *Outline*, intending to make a "Book of Necessary Knowledge" that would sum up the achievement of humankind and take a first step toward creating what he called "The Mind of the Race." Wells never gave up his encyclopedic ambitions. In 1936 he proposed a "World Brain," a storehouse of human knowledge: "As mankind is, so will it remain until it pulls its mind together."

Wells continued to support his notion of a World State in imaginative projections of Utopias, ideal ways of living that might be created if only men would use their reason instead of their worst instincts.

In creating his ideal societies, Wells was writing in a long tradition, stretching from his favorite Plato's *Republic* and Sir Thomas More's *Utopia* (1516) to Samuel

Wells in 1919: he was now determined to use his writing powers to create a united world and a lasting peace.

Butler's *Erewhon* (1872) and William Morris's *News from Nowhere* (1891). A particular influence on him was Winwood Reade's Victorian classic, *The Martyrdom of Man*, which ended with an optimistic vision of the future.

> Earth, which is now a purgatory, will be made a paradise . . . by the efforts of man himself. Hunger and starvation will then be unknown and the earth will be a garden. [Man] will repress the base instincts . . . which he has inherited from the animals below . . . he will worship the divinity within him . . . Men will look upon this star as their fatherland: its progress will be their ambition, the gratitude of others their reward. Finally men will master the forces of nature, they will themselves become architects of systems, manufacturers of worlds.
>
> (Winwood Reade, *The Martyrdom of Man*, 1872)

Wells writes of the Utopias that he imagined with a genuine longing, as if he ached to belong to that better world. "That World State of more vivid, beautiful, and eventful people is, so to speak on the brow of the hill," he had claimed years before, in a lecture of 1902, "and we cannot see over, though some of us can imagine great uplands beyond and something, something that

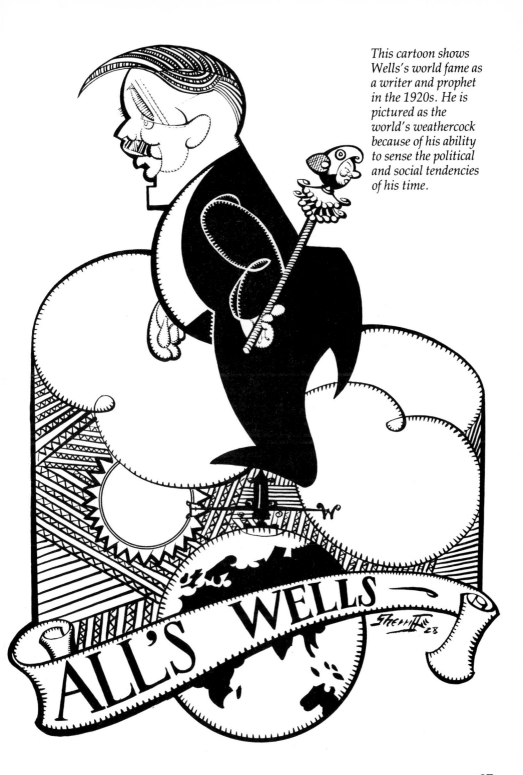

This cartoon shows Wells's world fame as a writer and prophet in the 1920s. He is pictured as the world's weathercock because of his ability to sense the political and social tendencies of his time.

ALL'S WELLS

glitters elusively, taking one form and then another through the haze."

Borrowing from the Guardians of Plato's *Republic*, Wells favored the idea of an élite that would guide humankind into a better future: the "Samurai" of *A Modern Utopia* were a first version of this idea. In the 1920s he proposed the "Open Conspiracy": creative people of intellect from all nations could come together to seize control of the world's resources in a quiet revolution that would form the basis of international government.

In *Men Like Gods* (1923), the most attractive and warmly colored of Wells's Utopias, there is no élite; the Utopians have passed far beyond the initial revolution and are all dedicated to sane, creative living. Mr. Barnstaple, a journalist, is suddenly transferred by a "space-warp" to Utopia, an ideal world in a parallel universe to our own. After exploring this world, he has to return to earth. There he resolves to work for a better order of living.

> Earth would tread the path Utopia had trod ... And as this great revolution was achieved and Earth wheeled into daylight, the burden of human miseries would lift, and courage cast sorrow from the hearts of men. Earth, which was now no more than a wilderness ... interspersed with weedy scratchings for food and with hovels and slums and slagheaps, Earth too would grow rich with loveliness and fair as this great land was fair. The sons of Earth also, purified from disease, sweet-minded and strong and beautiful, would go proudly about their conquered planet and lift their daring to the stars ...
>
> (*Men Like Gods*, Book 4, Ch. 3)

The Shape of Things to Come (1933) is a history book of the future, supposedly imagined in a dream. A final terrible war, starting in 1940 on the German–Polish border and employing devastating chemical and gas weapons, is followed by a "wave of sanity" that creates the World State. In the movie *Things to Come*, produced by Alexander Korda in 1936, the story is still very exciting, with its memorable scenes of war, social collapse and reconstruction set to the powerful music of Arthur Bliss. However, the film's conclusion, described by Beatrice Webb as "masses of moving machinery [and] multitudes of men and women ... scurrying about like ants," has none of the mellow splendor of Wells's original book, the final chapters of which show people freed from poverty, illness and war able to devote themselves to creative activity.

When we have had enough of our own work for a time we fly off to see what other people are doing. The world is full of interest and delight, from the forest gardens of the Amazons with their sloths, monkeys and occasional pumas and alligators to that playground of the world, the snowfields of the Himalayas. We can arrange to take a turn with the meteorological observers in the upper air, or tune our lungs for a spell in the deep sea galleries below the rafts of Atlantis ...

In the spectacular 1936 movie Things to Come, *a devastating world war is followed by a progressive, science-orientated civilization led by the "Airmen." One such black-uniformed, gas-helmeted Airman is seen in this still.*

Men become more curious, more excited, more daring, skilful and pleasantly occupied each year . . . This planet, which seemed so stern a mother to mankind, is discovered to be inexhaustible in its bounty. And the greatest discovery man has made is the discovery of himself. Leonardo da Vinci with his immense breadth of vision, his creative fervour, his curiosity, his power of intensive work, was the precursor of the ordinary man, as the world is now producing him.

(*The Shape of Things to Come*, Book 5)

Such a vision can still be inspiring half a century later when every newspaper still mirrors what Wells called a sickening "Age of Confusion."

Whatever his daydreams of a better world, Wells's own life was increasingly unhappy in the inter-war years. His wealth brought him little contentment, even if it did buy him several houses, including a retreat in

The cartoonist, Low, pictured Wells's unflagging vigor during the 1930s.

Wells's seventieth birthday caused him to look back on his life, and one result of this was his Experiment in Autobiography.

the South of France where he lived "like minor royalty." When his wife died in 1927, the loneliness of advancing age began. He became retrospective; the researches of his official biographer, Geoffrey West, stimulated Wells to write his own *Experiment in Autobiography* (1934), the first volume of which has the same fascination as his best social novels.

In 1936 a host of friends met to celebrate his seventieth birthday. In a speech Wells compared himself to "a little boy ... who has been given quite a lot of jolly toys ... Then comes his nurse. 'Now, Master Bertie,' she says, 'it's getting late. Time you began to put away your toys.'" He concluded poignantly: "I hate the thought of leaving ... few of my games are nearly finished and some I feel are hardly begun."

Wells became frustrated that his ideas about world unity were largely ignored. In 1934 he visited President F.D. Roosevelt of the United States and Joseph Stalin, dictator of the U.S.S.R., seeing them as possible agents for his Open Conspiracy. Neither listened to his arguments. "Though most of the people of the world in key positions are more or less accessible to me, I lack the solvent power to bring them in unison," he wrote sadly. "I can talk to them, and even unsettle them, but I cannot compel their brains to see."

In the darkening world of the late 1930s, with economic depression and fascist dictatorships as frightening realities, Wells's Utopian dreams appeared impractical. Beatrice Webb wrote in her diary after a meeting with Wells: "He was obsessed with his own vague vision of world order. He ignored the problems of race and

Wells leaving Waterloo Station in London on his way to meet President F. D. Roosevelt in the United States in 1934.

religion, of rights and sexual habits . . . Of industry and agriculture, commerce and finance he knows nothing. Poor old Wells." George Orwell, a writer of growing importance who had been deeply influenced by Wells in his youth, described his disillusion with him: "The singleness of mind, the one-sided imagination that made him seem like an inspired prophet in the Edwardian

In 1934 Wells also visited the leader of the U.S.S.R., Joseph Stalin, to discuss his ideas for a World State.

Age, make him a shallow, inadequate thinker now."
In the face of Hitler's terror, Wells could offer only
"the usual rigmarole about the world state." In self-pity,
Wells came to see himself as another Roger Bacon (the

Hitler's Nazis at a rally in Germany in the 1930s. Later George Orwell attacked Wells as an out-of-date figure who had had nothing to say about Hitler's regime of terror.

medieval thinker and prophet), "a man altogether lonely and immediately futile, a man lit by a vision of a world still some centuries ahead, convinced of its reality and urgency, and yet powerless to bring it nearer."

6
Darkening
Visions

Wells lived his final years during the tremendous drama of World War II. In the summer of 1939, just before Britain declared war on Germany, he painted a grim picture of the coming conflict.

> It will be the Dark Ages over again, a planetary instead of a European Dark Ages ... Mankind, which began in a cave and behind a windbreak, will end in the disease-soaked ruins of a slum.
>
> (*The Fate of Homo Sapiens*, 1939)

Wells continued to travel widely to speak about world events, even after the outbreak of World War II in 1939.

In 1940 while on fire-watching duty near his house by Regent's Park, Wells contemplated the glare and thunder of the real London Blitz and composed, with a kind of satisfaction, his own epitaph: "I told you so! You damned fools!"

Despite increasing illness, which finally limited his worldwide travels, he continued to write, concerning himself with a "Declaration of the Rights of Man" as a basis for Allied war aims. His still extensive journalism irritated many people. His attacks on the Catholic Church and the British Monarchy (as institutions that stood in the way of his World State) were widely resented. Not surprisingly, he did not receive any state honors. The only honor he really coveted was a Fellowship of the Royal Society. In the hope of receiving a fellowship, Wells prepared a thesis for an advanced degree and became Doctor of Science in 1943. Despite these efforts, he was not elected to the Society; this was a bitter disappointment for Wells.

On fire-watching duty during the London Blitz of 1940, Wells grimly noted that he had foretold aerial bombing in The War in the Air *in 1908.*

Wells lived to see the first atomic bomb attack on Japan in 1945. He began to plan another version of his 1936 movie success, *Things to Come*, to fit the atomic age – this new "grave and tragic" human situation. In his last

housebound months with his mind darkened by illness, Wells reverted to the pessimism of his youth, when he had imagined in *The Time Machine* "this earth of ours . . . dead and frozen, and all that lived upon it . . . frozen

In 1945 Wells began to plan another version of his movie Things to Come.

out and done with." In the powerful, fragmentary work *Mind at the End of its Tether* (1945), he again predicted the extinction of the human race. Evoking the mood of "the later, brooding Shakespeare," who saw life as "a tale told by an idiot . . . signifying nothing," Wells asserted that:

Homo Sapiens in his present form is played out. The stars in their courses have turned against him and he has to give place to some other animal better adapted to face the fate that closes in more and more swiftly upon mankind . . . The cinema sheet stares us in the face . . . Our loves, our hates, our wars and battles are no more than a phantasmagoria dancing on that fabric, themselves as unsubstantial as a dream . . . There is no way out or through the impasse. It is the end.

(Mind at the End of its Tether, 1945)

The book is completed by seven short anecdotes that comment bitterly on men as "the most foolish vermin that have ever over-run the earth." "The Culminating Man" is one of these. As the earth dies, one greedy, selfish individual escapes death, until God's angel breaks into his survival shelter:

The cold air of eternal righteousness blew in upon him, and forthwith he and all his gettings and belongings shrivelled into a slimy powder and evaporated to nothing. "Homo Sapiens" he used to call himself, said the inquiring Seraph, and turned his mind to other matters . . .

(Mind at the End of its Tether)

Wells died on August 13, 1946, one month short of his eightieth birthday. He was hailed by his friend, the playwright and novelist J. B. Priestley, as "one of the major prophets of this age . . . whose word was light in a thousand dark places . . . The greatness was there; the wide range, the sudden flash of insight [and] lighting up everything he did, the selfless passion for the welfare of the whole troubled species."

Glossary

Anecdote   A brief story of amusing or interesting incident.

Cyclical   Recurring in cycles.

Dictatorship   Rule by one person.

Draper   A dealer in cloth or dry goods.

Élite   Select group or class.

Emporium   Large general store or market center.

Evolution   Nineteenth-century scientific theory, proposed by Charles Darwin, that species change gradually by development from earlier forms.

Fable   Story that contains a lesson or message.

Fin de siècle   (Literally "end of the century") mood of decay and decline felt at the end of the nineteenth century.

Futurology   Study of the future.

Genre   A style or category within literature (i.e. science fiction).

Grammar school   A secondary school, especially one in which Latin and Greek are taught.

Headmaster   Principal of a school.

Irony   Grimly humorous twist in events.

Phantasmagoria   Shifting scene of real or imaginary figures.

Prototype   First version.

Satire   Use of ridicule to attack a fault or weakness in a person or a society.

Scientific romance   Victorian genre name for the science fiction novel.

Seminal   Idea that gives basis for future development.

Sociology   Study of society.

Syndicated   Published simultaneously in several newspapers.

Theme   General idea raised by a work of literature.

Topography   Natural and manmade features of a district.

Utopia From two Greek works meaning "no place." Particularly, it was the title given by Sir Thomas More to his famous book of 1516. Generally, the term is now used of any study of an imaginary, ideal society. The Athenian philosopher Plato (*c.* 427–347 B.C.) discussed the idea of an ideal state in his *Republic*.

Yahoo Beast-like human beings. (Term invented by Jonathan Swift in *Gulliver's Travels*, 1726.)

List of Dates

	Life
1866	September 21: Born at Bromley, Kent.
1873–80	Educated at Morley's Academy, Bromley.
1880	Mother becomes housekeeper at Uppark, Sussex. Wells leaves school to enter drapery trade in Windsor.
1880–81	Stays with mother at Uppark. Reads Jonathan Swift, Tom Paine and Plato.
1881	January: Becomes pharmacist's apprentice at Midhurst, Sussex. Takes Latin lessons at Midhurst Grammar School. May: Becomes apprentice draper at Southsea, Hampshire.
1883	Revolts against drapery. Becomes pupil-teacher at Midhurst Grammar School.
1884	Wins scholarship to Normal School of Science, South Kensington. Studies under T. H. Huxley.
1887	Leaves Normal School of Science without degree. Takes up a teaching post in Wales. Has a kidney injury. Returns to Uppark.
1888	Returns to London seeking work.
1889	Accepts a teaching post at Henley House School, in north London.
1890	Finishes BSc degree. Studies for teaching qualifications. Accepts a post at university correspondence college.
1891	Marries his cousin, Isabel.
1893	Health breaks down. Gives up teaching. First journalistic successes. Elopes with Catherine Robbins.
1895	Divorces Isabel. Marries Catherine.
1898	Health collapses. Moves to Sandgate, Kent.
1900	Moves into Spade House, Sandgate.
1903	Joins the Fabian Society.
1906	Challenges for leadership of Fabians. Visits the United States.
1909	*Ann Veronica* creates a scandal.
1912	Moves to Easton Glebe, Dunmow, Essex.
1914	Outbreak of World War I (1914–18).
1919	Works for League of Nations idea.
1920	Visits the U.S.S.R. Meets Lenin.
1926	Builds Lou Pidou, a house in France.

1927	Catherine Wells dies.
1928	Proposes the "Open Conspiracy," a plan for quiet revolution leading to World State.
1929	Moves to London.
1934	Visits President Roosevelt and Joseph Stalin.
1938	*The War of the Worlds* is broadcast in the United States causing panic.
1939	Outbreak of World War II (1939–45). Works on "Declaration of the Rights of Man."
1946	August 13: H. G. Wells dies.

Works

1887	*The Chronic Argonauts*
1895	*The Time Machine*
	The Wonderful Visit
1896	*The Island of Dr. Moreau*
	The Wheels of Chance
1897	*The Invisible Man*
1898	*The War of the Worlds*
1899	*A Story of the Days to Come*
	When the Sleeper Wakes (later renamed *The Sleeper Awakes*)
1900	*Love and Mr. Lewisham*
1901	*The First Men in the Moon*
	Anticipations
1903	"The Land Ironclads"
1904	*The Food of the Gods*
1905	*A Modern Utopia*
	Kipps
1906	*In the Days of the Comet*
	"The Door in the Wall"
1908	*The War in the Air*
1909	*Ann Veronica*
	Tono-Bungay
1910	*The History of Mr. Polly*
1911	*The New Machiavelli*
1912	"The Country of the Blind" (stories)
1914	*The World Set Free*
	"The war that will end war"
1916	*Mr. Britling Sees It Through*
1918	*Joan and Peter*
1919–20	*The Outline of History*
1923	*Men Like Gods*
1933	*The Shape of Things to Come*
1934	*Experiment in Autobiography*
1936	*Things to Come* (movie)
1939	*The Fate of Homo Sapiens*
1945	*Mind at the End of its Tether*

Further Reading

Biography

HAMMOND, J.R. *H.G.Wells: Interviews and Recollections* (Macmillan, 1980)

MACKENZIE, N. & J. *The Time Traveller: the Life of H. G. Wells* (Weidenfeld & Nicolson, 1973) (new edition 1987)

SMITH, D.H. *H.G.Wells: Desperately Mortal* (Yale University Press, 1986)

WELLS, Frank *H.G.Wells: A Pictorial Biography* (Jupiter Books, 1978)

WELLS, H.G. *Experiment in Autobiography* (Victor Gollancz, 1934; Cresset Press, 1966)

WEST, Anthony *H.G.Wells: Aspects of a Life* (Hutchinson, 1984/Penguin, 1985)

WEST, Geoffrey *H.G.Wells: A Sketch for a Portrait* (Gerald Howe, 1930)

Individual novels

The most popular books are constantly reprinted as paperbacks by various publishers. Several of the lesser-known books have also been reprinted recently.

Collected editions

Complete Science Fiction Treasury of H.G.Wells (Averel Books, 1978)

Complete Short Stories of H.G.Wells (Benn/St Martin's Library 1927, reprinted 1979)

HAINING, P. *The H.G.Wells Scrapbook* (New English Library, 1979)

HAMMOND, J. (ed.) *The Man with the Nose, etc.* (early stories) (Athlone, 1984)

H.G.Wells Omnibus (science fiction novels) (Heinemann/Octopus, 1977)

PARRINDER, P. & PHILMUS, R. *H.G.Wells: Literary Criticism* (Harvester, 1980)

PHILMUS, R. & HUGHES, D. *H.G.Wells: Early Writings in Science and Science Fiction* (University of California Press, 1975)

Selected Short Stories (Penguin 1958: often reprinted)
WARREN WAGAR, W. *H. G. Wells: Journalism and Prophecy 1893–1946* (Bodley Head, 1964)

Critical works

BATCHELOR, J. *H. G. Wells* (Cambridge University Press, 1985)

BERGONZI, B. (ED.) *H. G. Wells: A Collection of Critical Essays* (Prentice Hall, 1976)

BERGONZI, B. *The Early H. G. Wells: A Study of the Scientific Romances* (University of Manchester Press, 1961)

HAMMOND, J. R. *An H. G. Wells Companion* (Macmillan Press, 1979)

HAYNES, R. D. *H. G. Wells: Discoverer of the Future* (Macmillan Press, 1979)

HILLEGAS, M. *The Future as Nightmare: H. G. Wells and the anti-Utopians* (Oxford, 1967)

McCONNELL, F. *The Science Fiction of H. G. Wells* (Oxford, 1981)

PARRINDER, P. (ED.) *H. G. Wells: the Critical Heritage* (Routledge, 1972)

PARRINDER, P. *H. G. Wells* (Oliver and Boyd, 1970)

RAKNEM, I. *H. G. Wells and his Critics* (Allen and Unwin, 1962)

WARREN WAGAR, W. *H. G. Wells and the World State* (Yale University Press, 1961)

Background reading

ASH, B. *Visual Encyclopaedia of Science Fiction* (Pan, 1977)

CLARKE, I. F. *The Pattern of Expectation 1649–2001* (Cape, 1979)

CLARKE, I. F. *Tales of the Future* (Bibliography) (Library Association, 1972)

CLARKE, I. F. *Voices Prophesying War 1773–1984* (Oxford, 1966)

EVANS, H. & D. *Beyond the Gaslight: Science in Popular Fiction* (Muller, 1975)

FREWIN, A. *100 Years of Science Fiction Illustration* (Hart-Davis, 1975)

GUNN, J. *Alternate Worlds: the Illustrated History of Science Fiction* (Prentice Hall, 1975)

KYLE, D. *A Pictorial History of Science Fiction* (Hamlyn, 1976)

WHEELER, M. & TODD, I. *Utopia: an Illustrated History* (Harmony, 1978)
WYKES, A. *H. G. Wells in the Cinema* (Jupiter, 1977)

Records
The War of the Worlds narrated by Richard Burton, music by Jeff Wayne (CBS 96000, two-record set with illustrated booklet)
Things to Come concert suite, Sir Arthur Bliss (music for 1936 film) (SDD 255 Decca)

Picture acknowledgments

The author and publishers would like to thank the following for allowing their illustrations to be reproduced in this book: Aquarius Picture Library 41, 44; the British Library 32; Bromley Public Library 7, 8, 9, 15, 21, 22, 25, 26, 27, 31; the Syndics of Cambridge University Library 11, 33, 43, 46, 49, 52, 53, 55, 56, 57, 62, 65, 72, 77, 79; Essex County Library 76; Mary Evans Picture Library 6, 20, 35, 36, 38, 39, 60, 68, 71, 74, 75, 78, 80, 83, 86, 90; John Frost 47; BBC Hulton Picture Library 93, 94; the University of Illinois Library 28, 29, 34, 42; Illustrated London News 63, 64, 100; the Mansell Collection 12, 59, 81; National Film Archive 50, 69, 89, 99; the National Trust 14, 17; National Portrait Gallery 87; Popperfoto 92, 96; Topham Picture Library 97; Charles White 19.

Index

figures in **bold** refer to illustrations

Copyright 1988 Wayland (Publishers) Ltd.
61 Western Road, Hove, East Sussex
BN3 1JD England